Summer Vacation

A Story About Patience

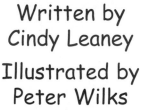
Written by
Cindy Leaney

Illustrated by
Peter Wilks

Rourke
Publishing LLC
Vero Beach, Florida 32964

Before you read this story, take a look at the front cover of the book. The two kids in the picture are Emily and José.

1. What are they doing?

2. Why do you think they are going to need to be patient?

Produced by SGA Illustration and Design
Designed by Phil Kay
Series Editor: Frank Sloan

www.rourkepublishing.com

Library of Congress Cataloging-in-Publication Data

Leaney, Cindy.
   Summer Vacation : patience / by Cindy Leaney ; illustrated by Peter Wilks.
      p. cm.-- (Hero club character)
   Summary: When José and his grandfather build a birdhouse and plant vegetable seeds together, José learns about the rewards of patience.
      ISBN 1-58952-737-2
      [1. Patience--Fiction. 2. Conduct of life--Fiction.] I. Wilks, Peter, ill. II. Title.

   PZ7.L46335Su2003
      [E]--dc21

                                                            2003043235

Printed in the USA
MP/W

Hi! I'm Makayla!

Hi! I'm Emily!

Hi! I'm Matt!

Hi! I'm José!

Welcome to The Hero Club!

Read about all the things that happen to them.

Try and guess what they'll do next.

www.theheroclub.com

"Wow. A whole summer. Let's go over to my grandpa's house."

"Excellent."

"Sounds good."

"What are we going to do today, Abuelo?"

"First we're going to build a birdhouse. When we finish that we can plant some seeds. I think you kids are old enough to have your own vegetable patch this year."

"Yay! Let's go to the store and buy seeds for our vegetable patch!"

"No, we need to get the birdhouse finished first."

"We'll cut out two rectangles for the roof. Then a front and a back wall.
Then two side walls and a floor.
Then we'll cut a hole for a door and put it all together.
Then we'll paint it."

"There! All done! Now we'll wait
for a pair of birds to move in."

"When will they come?"

"Oh, in about three or four weeks. They won't come until our smell is gone."

"Three or four weeks!"

"Let's plant the seeds!"

14

"First we need to plant them in a tray.
Then we can rake the soil and get
everything ready."

"Radishes, beans, and pumpkins. Let's see. You should have radishes in a month or so. And your pumpkins will be ready for Halloween."

"Halloween! Abue, why does everything take so long?"

"It doesn't really. It just seems to."

"My mom says time goes more slowly for kids."

"She's right."

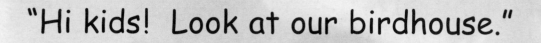

"Hi kids! Look at our birdhouse."

"The eggs hatched!
I can hear the baby birds."

"Awesome!"

"Look, Abue!
We've got tiny pumpkins!"

"Those are going to be good ones."

"It's been a great summer, hasn't it?"

"Abue, this was the best summer ever."

"Was it worth being patient and waiting for all those things?"

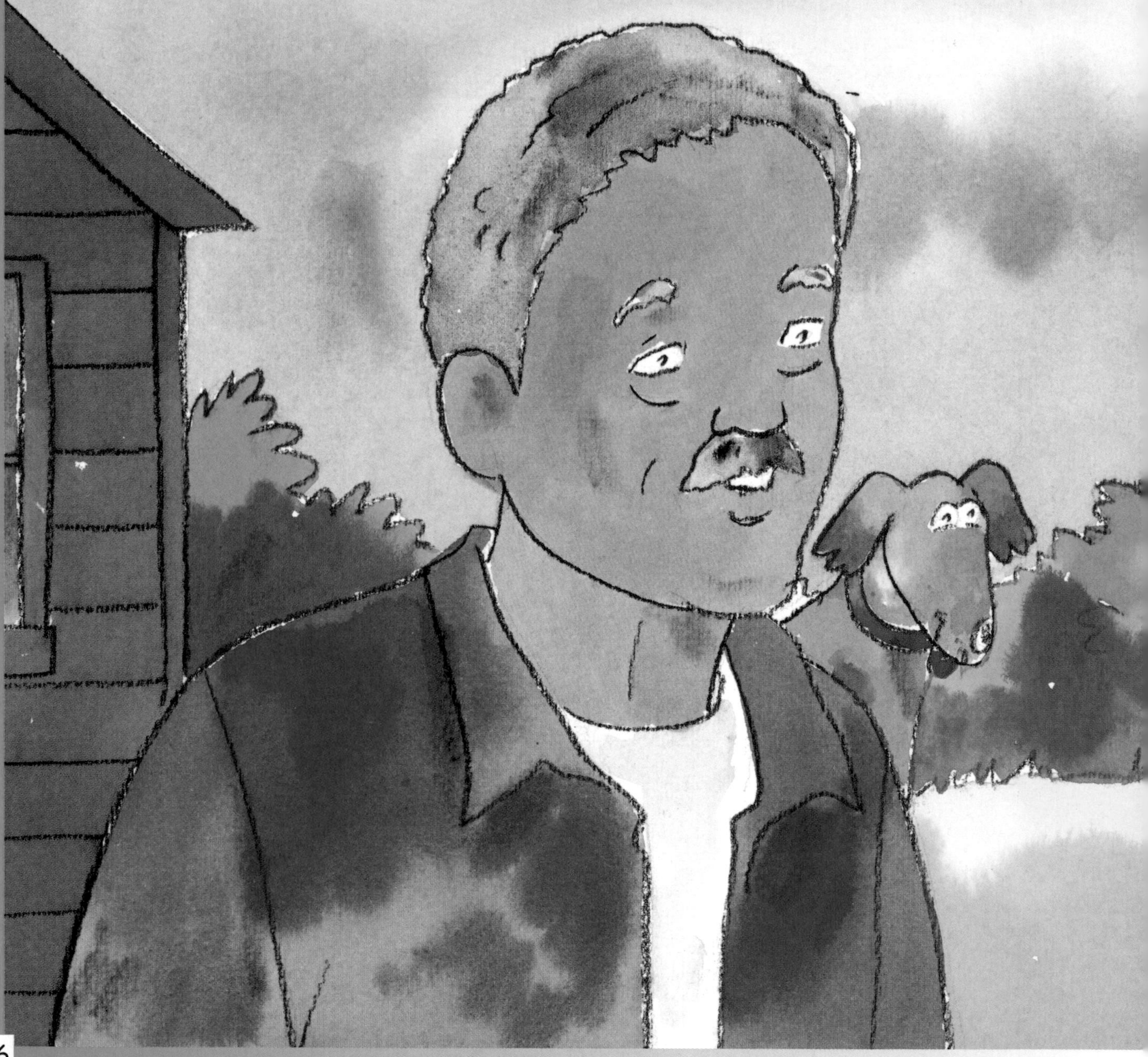

"And thanks for being patient with us!"

WHAT DO YOU THINK?

When did José have to be patient? What good things happened because the kids were patient?

IMPORTANT IDEAS

Patience – When you have patience, you stay calm and do not get angry if you have to wait for a long time or do something that is difficult or complicated. On page

26, José's grandfather says, "Was it worth being patient and waiting for all those things?"

The opposite of patient is impatient.

Do you ever have to be patient with people or wait for things to happen?

Now that you have read this book, see if you can answer these questions:

1. What kinds of projects do the Hero Club kids do at Grandfather's house?

2. What steps were involved in planting the seeds?

3. What kinds of seeds did the Hero Club kids plant? And which grew the fastest?

About the author

Cindy Leaney teaches English and writes books for both young readers and adults. She has lived and worked in England, Kenya, Mexico, Saudi Arabia, and the United States.

About the illustrator

Peter Wilks began work in advertising, where he developed a love for illustration. He has drawn pictures for many children's books in Great Britain and in the United States.

HERO CLUB CHARACTER VALUE SERIES

Everyone Makes a Difference (A Book About Community)

Field Trip (A Book About Sharing)

It's Your Turn Now (A Book About Politeness)

Lost and Found (A Book About Honesty)

Summer Vacation (A Book About Patience)

Taking Care of Mango (A Book About Responsibility)